# RANGER BALDY
### and the
## DISAPPEARING WATERFALL

A Yosemite National Park Adventure

By Ranger Baldy, himself
Illustrated by Natalie Long

Translated from Eaglish by Stephen Zapotoczny.

Published by The Magic Factory, LLC, Los Angeles, California.
For contact information, visit MagicFactory.com

Printed in the United States of America.
ISBN 978-1-938155-00-0
Library of Congress Control Number: 2013932447

First Edition
10 9 8 7 6 5 4 3 2 1
LPH

Copyright © 2013 by Stephen Zapotoczny
All rights reserved.

THIS LABEL APPLIES TO TEXT STOCK

*For Myles and Matthew,
the first to hear my adventures.*

My name's Baldy – Ranger Baldy –
Animal Ranger Corps, Ranger First Class.

One late summer day, I was patrolling high over California's Yosemite (yo-SEH-mih-tee) Valley on the lookout for trouble. For rangers, trouble is one of those things you're always looking for, but hope you never find.

I'd only been in Yosemite a short time, but the valley already felt like home. The local animals called it "The Valley of the Great Falls," for it was just that – a flat forest surrounded by high mountain cliffs and lots of towering waterfalls.

"Help!" a young voice cried out below.

I scanned the valley floor. Bobby Cat was clinging to a branch that overhung the swimming hole at the bottom of the tallest waterfall. He'd climbed too high again.

My old Ranger Chief said the little things mattered most when stopping trouble, helping out, or protecting the land. This was a little thing. I wanted to keep it that way.

I dived toward Bobby. Another sound, like the slow cracking of ice, filled the sky.
"The branch!" yelled Bobby. "It's break–"
SNAP!

Not just the branch, but the entire tree, fell. I caught Bobby mid-air, but the tree smashed against the mountain, setting off a chain reaction. One by one, trees toppled into each other.

Above the swimming hole, where the water spilled over the rocks, the last tree fell. It knocked a boulder into the river and with a gurgle, the waterfall stopped.
*Trouble!*

"Thanks, Ranger Baldy," said Bobby, as we landed. His pal, Mules Deer, was just climbing out of the swimming hole. I inspected the destruction. If I'd rescued Bobby sooner, the fall would still be flowing. The little thing had mattered.

"You damaged sacred land," I growled, dusting off my badge and adjusting my hat like I'd seen the toughest lawmen do. "Land I've sworn to protect."

"It was an accident," replied Bobby.

"When you cause the accident, you fix the mess," I said. "Let's move that boulder."

I flew to the top of the cliff, while Bobby and Mules scampered up the mountain trail.

The three of us nudged the boulder until the stream began to flow around it. The waterfall started...

...then stopped again.

"Not good," I said. "I'll fly upstream and investigate. Don't climb any trees!"
The friends nodded.

I followed the curve of the stream up the mountain. It was almost dry.
Strange.
What had caused the water to disappear? The youngsters? Or something worse?
Then I spotted a clue on the stream bank – two-legger prints.

Two-leggers had a way of destroying things. They'd cut forests, dammed rivers, and polluted the air. I'd been born in a zoo since they'd ruined my parent's forest home. When I was set free, I joined the Animal Ranger Corps to protect Earth's treasures from those who might harm them, and two-leggers were at the top of my list.

Were two-leggers to blame for the dry streambed?

Their trail led into the ancient forest, home to Earth's largest living things, the Giant Sequoia trees.

I touched down to study the prints. Graycee Fox emerged from her nearby den. "Tracking something, ranger?" she asked.

"Two-leggers," I replied. "The great fall's disappeared and the stream's run dry."

"I saw the two-leggers, dear. They were caring for these babies." She pawed some fragile Sequoia saplings. "But without water, I'm afraid the trees won't survive."

The two-legger's good deed surprised me, but I was still suspicious. The stream was still dry, trouble was still trouble, and precious time was ticking away.

"I'll find water," I said.

Fast as my wings carried me, I flew back into the valley to fetch water from another of the grand waterfalls. But where each waterfall once flowed, there was nothing more than a trickle. *All the water was missing!*

The mess was far worse than I'd imagined. On my watch, The Valley of the Great Falls had become an ordinary valley.

Discouraged, I landed in a field.
"Sssssssstep off The King!" hissed a high-pitched voice.
I jumped back. A king snake curled up from the grass.
"Sorry, sire," I said. I'd meant no harm.
"Sssssssire? Sssssssire!" said the snake. "I am The King, but I am no SSSSSSSIRE!"

I turned to leave, but froze. Before me, hidden in the grass, was a nest of snake eggs.

So The King wasn't a *sire*. The King was a *she*, not a *he* – a *mother!* The problem with snakes is you can't tell the difference.

"Sorry, Ma'am," I said, dipping my hat. "Let's find a safer place for your youngsters."

The King smiled as I gently moved her nest to an old burrow nearby. I'd been wrong about her. I'd been wrong about the two-leggers. Was there a clue I'd been missing too? My investigation needed a fresh start.

I climbed toward the clouds. The King's babies would need a drink when they hatched. I was more determined than ever to find that water.

Cleft Rock – *Half Dome* as I'd heard a two-legger call it – was the perfect place to look for new clues. Perched there, searching the wilderness, I noticed something strange.
The high country was *too* green...
It wasn't just water that was missing.

Snow was missing too.
*Could this be the clue I'd been searching for?*
My old Ranger Chief, J.M. Bear, lived in the high country. It was time to pay him a visit.

I found J.M. foraging for food in the big meadow.
"To what do I owe the pleasure?" he asked.
"Snow," I replied.
"Melted yesterday. Why?"
"Trouble's reared its ugly head. Water's disappeared. The great falls are dry."

J.M. just laughed. "That's not trouble," he said. "It's Mother Nature's magic. Every autumn, when the snow up here disappears, so does the valley's water. And every spring it returns with the new melt."

So melted snow from the high country fed streams and falls in the valley below. *No snow meant no water!*

"Take my badge," I said, yanking it off. "I should've known. A good ranger always knows."

"No. A good ranger searches until he finds answers," said J.M. "You did that. And I'm sure you even helped some folks along the way."

I remembered Bobby, Mules, Miss Graycee and The King, then nodded.

"It's those little things that matter most," said J.M. "They make the big difference."

My old friend was right. I'd done my duty. I smiled and replaced my badge. After saying goodbye, I fetched water from a nearby mountain lake for Miss Graycee's saplings and The King's youngsters, then took off for the valley to tell Bobby and Mules about my discovery.

A few weeks later, Mother Nature worked a little more magic. An autumn snowstorm covered The Valley of the Great Falls with a thick blanket of white powder. Shimmering icicles dangled from high stone outcroppings.

Water had returned. The falls would flow again. Trouble was officially gone!